2021

WHISPERS FROM HEAVEN

PAIGE SQUIRRELL

(a friend)

KINGDOM BREAKTHROUGH
Ministries

CONTENTS

INTRODUCTION

'My heart has heard you say, "Come and talk with me." And my heart responds, "Lord, I am coming."'

— PSALM 27:8

'Oh Lord, you're beautiful. Your face is all I seek.'

There's no better way to live than to seek the Lord's face and to be constantly connected to the One who created us and knows us better than anyone else. It's when we are in His presence that we are transformed. In His presence we become like Him. In His presence we find our true identity and our reason for being.

We live in a noisy world full of different voices shouting at us, vying for our undivided attention, creating confusion and frustration. In the midst of all the noise, it is possible to tune in and hear our Father whisper, 'Come to me.' He deserves our undivided attention. His voice brings life, order, purpose, and peace.

May these whispers encourage your heart and bring you joy. The Father wants to speak to you and encourage your heart. He wants to be your glory and the lifter of your head.

After each whisper, you will find declarations and a prayer. Proverbs 18:20-21 reminds us that 'Wise words satisfy like a good meal; the right words bring satisfaction. The tongue can bring death or life; those who love to talk will reap the consequences.' The words we speak are important. They have the power to release life or death to our own lives and the situations we face. Jesus said His words were Spirit and life. What better example to follow than Jesus Himself.

Making declarations, a habit I cherish, has completely transformed my mind, the way I view myself, others, and life. Declaring truth is powerful. It is my hope that the declaration after each whisper will inspire you and act as a springboard to take God's beautiful, Holy Spirit inspired words and turn them into your own declaration. You will soon notice significant changes in you and as a result you will begin to effect change around you.

Enjoy your journey with Father God.

DAY 1

My grace is all you need today. My power works best in your weakness. My dear child, don't focus on your weaknesses and inadequacies today. Focus on me. I am your strength. Don't focus on what I am not doing. Focus on what I am doing and give thanks. My grace will never run out. There will always be enough for each day. Give thanks and watch my grace increase in your life. My grace is like the manna I provided for the Israelites in the wilderness. They had to collect it fresh every day. It couldn't be stored for another day. Look for my grace today. Grace is my gift to you. Receive it. Let it work in you. Give me your weakness and I'll give you grace in return. My grace will work through you in power. I see you and I am for you. I love you and I want the best for you. My grace will be enough for today and tomorrow there will be more grace. There's no need to worry. You can rest in my sufficient grace day by day. My grace is my power and strength at work in you enabling you to live moment by moment.

(2 Corinthians 12:9-10; Hebrews 4:16)

DECLARATIONS

- *God's grace is enough for me today.*
- *I am not defined by my weaknesses. I walk in God's power.*
- *I will not strive but rest in God's amazing grace.*
- *Because I have received God's grace, I can give grace wherever I go.*
- *God's grace enables me to accomplish all that He has for me to do.*

PRAYER

Thank you, Lord, that your grace will enable me to walk in power today. Thank you that where I am weak, your strength will take over. As I look to you, you will work in and through me. I choose to rest in you and to no longer partner with striving.

My name is your strong tower. My name is your strong fortress today. Run to me and you will be safe. I can understand you wanting to run to other sources. I can understand you being completely focussed on your needs. But that will never support you. Instead of running to other sources looking for what you need, run to me and you will find the source of your 'enough'. My pool of resources never runs dry. There's always enough protection, enough provision, and enough nourishment to see my promises fulfilled in your life. I am your source of peace. I am your source of wisdom. I am your source of joy. I am your source of life. I am your source of hope. Run to me and you will experience safety. Run to me and you will experience provision. Run to me and you will experience my 'enough' in your life. My presence is a place where your needs are met. Run to me. I am waiting with my arms open ready to embrace you with my 'enough'. Run to me. I delight in you, my dear child, and I will never change. This source will always be here for you in my presence. I will never disappoint you. Run to me. Come close and you will find your deepest needs met.

(Psalm 91; Proverbs 18:10; Hebrews 13:8)

DECLARATIONS

- *The name of the Lord is my strong tower. I run to Him and I am safe.*
- *The Lord is my source of life, joy, and peace today.*
- *The Lord richly supplies all my needs.*
- *He is the same yesterday, today, and forever. He never changes.*
- *I can do and be all that I need to do and be through Him who gives me strength.*

PRAYER

Lord, thank you that you are enough. Thank you that your resources will never run out. Thank you that I have everything I need today to do life well.

DAY 3

You are my beloved and I am yours. Look to me today. Fix your eyes on me because I am your help. I will not let you stumble today. I watch over you and I never fall asleep on the job. My eye is on the sparrow and it is on you, too, 24/7. I see everything. I know everything. I stand beside you as your protective shade. Come and shelter in my shade. You will be safe. Come and sing in my shade. Know that I watch over you as you come and go today, tomorrow, the next day and every day of your life. You have reason to sing because nothing misses my attention. My eye is firmly fixed on you. I am your refuge and your shield. My words of truth and love are your source of hope. My Spirit flows through your very veins giving you power today to walk in my ways, to think my thoughts, to say my words, and to share my glory wherever you go today. You are mine and I love you. You are precious to me.

(Psalm 119; 121; Luke 12:6-7, 22-32; Colossians 1:27)

DECLARATIONS

- *The Lord is my strength, my refuge, and my shield.*
- *The Lord sees me, knows me, and loves me.*
- *The words of the Lord are spirit and life to me.*
- *I walk in the power of His Spirit today.*
- *His praise will be on my lips.*

PRAYER

Lord, thank you that I am your precious child safe in your presence today. Thank you that I have reason to sing to and praise you because nothing that happens today will miss your attention. Thank you that your eyes are on me and I can walk in complete power and confidence.

Y ou are my prized possession, my beautiful work of art placed where you are today for such a time as this. I am fulfilling my purposes in and through you. Come and worship me today. Turn your eyes on me so I can reveal my beauty and glory to you. I am still looking for worshippers, those who love me and give weight to who I am. Worshippers make the best workers for my Kingdom. Allow me to love you. Receive my love. Only then will you be able to love me. You love me and worship me with the love I give to you. Open your heart to my love. Receive my love. Then and only then will your roots grow down deep in me and you won't be shaken. Your life will be built on the Rock of my Son and you will be safe and secure. You will be made complete. Your faith will grow and you will overflow with my goodness and love for the people I bring to you. So come, receive my love. Let me surprise you with real satisfaction, contentment, and fulfilment, which can only come from being in my presence. My child, I love you. You are my prized possession and I want to be part of all you say and do today. Come to me. Enjoy my love. Live a life of worship.

(Psalm 17:15; John 4; Colossians 2:6-7)

DECLARATIONS

- *I am God's work of art created for good works today.*
- *I worship the Father with my words, thoughts, and actions.*
- *I choose to let the roots of my life grow down deep in the Father's love. In Him I am complete.*
- *Because of the Father's love for me, I will not be shaken by what comes my way.*
- *I choose to partner with God's perfect love and not with fear. His love surrounds me. It protects me. It fills me leaving no room for fear.*

PRAYER

Lord, thank you that you alone will satisfy and fulfil me today. My contentment is found in you and you alone. Thank you that your perfect love gets rid of all fear in my life. Fear no longer defines me but your love does.

'A peaceful heart leads to a healthy body.' Proverbs 14:30

I want you to know my peace today in a way that you haven't known it before. Peace I give to you. Receive my peace with open hands. Speak 'peace be still' to all your disappointments, confusion, turmoil, discouragement, hurts and fears. 'Peace be still!' I love you and I am in control of today. I have already won the victory for you today. Receive it and walk in it. I have the final word!! 'Peace be still!' I am the God of what was, what is, and what is to come! 'Peace be still'. Take your hands off the control button of your life. Relax and rest in the knowledge that I am your God. I will guard your heart and your mind today. My peace is a gift to you that the world could never give you. So don't go looking for it in places it cannot be found. Look to me. Give me the heavy weight of pressures, disappointments, questions, fears, frustrations, stresses and strains. It is only robbing you of the true life I came to bring. My peace opens the door to life; an enhanced life; an abundant life; life as I have designed and intended for you. Come, enter this beautiful exchange I have for you: my perfect peace for all that is weighing you down today.

DECLARATIONS

- *Jesus, you are my Prince of Peace.*
- *I receive your peace.*
- *Your peace will protect my mind, body, emotions, and family today.*
- *I speak "Peace be still" over my mind, body, emotions, family, and decisions I have to make.*
- *I am protected, strengthened, and made healthy by your peace.*

PRAYER

Jesus, thank you that you are Peace. Thank you that you are with me today releasing peace wherever I go. Thank you that I can experience peace and find rest in the midst of pressures because you are Peace. I receive your perfect peace.

DAY 6

'The Lord is my light and my salvation - so why should I be afraid? The Lord is my fortress, protecting me from danger, so why should I tremble?' Psalm 27:1

Live as my beloved child today. You are my adopted child, not an orphan or a slave controlled by fear. I chose you and I bought your freedom. You are no longer bound by fear. You are no longer bound by fear of circumstances. You are no longer bound by fear of what others might think or say. My very presence breaks the chains of fear. Because I am love, my presence releases love and sweeps away all fear, even those fears that are hidden. My love reaches to all the corners of your life and brings release and healing. Look to me today, trust me, and know that I am working everything out for your good. I make no mistakes. I am your good Father and I love you. You have my Spirit in you. You are my personal carrier of love, hope, light, and life to others. You are mine and I am yours. You are secure in my hands. I am your light and your salvation today. I am your fortress. You will not be overcome by fear. Be overcome by my love and allow it to wash over you. Together we will overcome today.

DECLARATIONS

- *I am a child of God with His light shining in me.*
- *I don't live in fear because the darkness around me cannot put out the light which is in me.*
- *God is love. He is my hope, my light, my salvation, my life.*
- *God is my deliverer.*
- *I walk in freedom today.*

PRAYER

Lord, thank you that I no longer need to live in fear. You are light and love. You are in me and I am in you. You take my fears and exchange them for your love. Thank you that you and I will overcome today. Nothing, absolutely nothing, will separate me from your incredible love today. I receive it now and choose to walk in the freedom it gives.

DAY 7

My precious child, I want you to know today that I care very deeply for you. No one else on this earth loves you and cares for you as deeply as I do. I hear every word you speak to me in prayer. It delights my heart to be in conversation with you. I bend down so that I can hear the silent cries of your heart. Every word, every thought, every cry, every question is important to me. You may not see answers to your prayers, cries, and questions right away but one thing you will always receive when you come into my presence is PEACE. Peace of mind. Peace of heart. Peace that conquers fear and anxiety. The world can't give you this peace. It is only found in relationship with me. Talk to me. Walk with me. Lean on me. Hold my hand. I will lead you down the path of peace. This path will never disappoint or overwhelm you. I never disappoint. I never overwhelm. I am always with you. You are too precious and important to me to let you carry those burdens. Give them to me and trust me. In trusting, you will receive peace. Remember, peace is a person. In trusting you, will receive me. I am your peace today.

(John 14:27; Psalm 116:1-2)

DECLARATIONS

- *I am kept in perfect peace because my trust is in God my Father.*
- *In Christ, I have a peace that passes all understanding. It is my gift for today.*
- *God's peace protects my mind and my heart so that disappointments no longer define me.*
- *I am a carrier of the peace God has given me.*
- *Peace reigns in me, in my home, and in all my circumstances.*

PRAYER

Father, thank you for your gift of peace. I receive it. Thank you that I don't need to live with disappointment or feelings of being overwhelmed. Thank you that your peace is protecting my mind and my heart so that I can live in a way that does your name proud today. Thank you that your peace will flow through me.

I am with you today. I so desire that you be aware of my presence every moment of today. It's when you're aware that I am with you, that you will be able to rise above your circumstances. Worry, fear, anxiety will flee as you thank me for my perfect peace, love, and joy. I am with you. Come up higher so you can see your day through my eyes. Acknowledge me and you will find rest and peace. Tune into my voice of love, purpose, and sense. I am with you and in you today and I will see you through today with all its ups and downs. Choose to trust me implicitly. Don't lean on your own understanding but lean on me. Lean on my words. Lean on my truth. Lean on my promises for you. Come to me. Give me what is weighing you down. Lean on me and let me take the weight. You don't need to carry it on your own. As you lean on me and begin to relax in my arms, strength will rise up in you. I am carrying you. My arms have got you and I will never put you down.

(Deuteronomy 33:26, 27, 29; Proverbs 3:5-8)

DECLARATIONS

- *Father God is with me today. He will never leave me or desert me.*
- *I am held in His arms.*
- *I can relax and rest today because His words are true and His promises are 'yes and amen' in Christ.*
- *God's peace defines me.*
- *I am a carrier the Father's perfect peace.*

PRAYER

Father, thank you that you are always with me. Thank you that your everlasting arms are underneath me and you will never grow weary of carrying me. Thank you that as I lean on you, you will take the weight of everything that is burdening me today. Thank you that your words and promises are true. Thank you that I can trust you and your wisdom and that as I do, I will receive healing for my body and strength for my bones.

It's easy to look at your day and only see the problems and the challenges. Even in the midst of them, it is possible to experience my peace and joy. Hold out your hands and receive my gifts. My peace will keep you from running away and retreating from what is happening today. My joy will sustain you through the problems and challenges. My peace will help you to embrace today and face the problems and challenges. My joy will help you to focus on what is important. I have given you my Son. He is your perfect High Priest and He is sitting next to me right now interceding for you. That is how important you are. He sees what you are facing and He is praying for you. Trust me. You will find peace and safety and with that will come joy. Delight yourself in me even with all the challenges whirling around you. Remember, I am the ONE who spoke and creation happened. I am the ONE who breathed and life was born. My SON spoke and the winds and waves submitted to Him. My SON spoke and blind eyes and deaf ears were opened. My SON spoke and the lame and sick were healed. Let us speak into your life today. Receive our words of life and hope. Let us breathe life and healing on you.

(Hebrews 7:25-28)

DECLARATIONS

- *The joy of the Lord is my strength. It is sustaining me in every situation.*
- *Jesus is my perfect High Priest interceding for me.*
- *I can face all the problems and challenges of today with peace and joy because greater is He who is in me than He who is in the world.*
- *I delight myself in the Lord. His praise will be on my lips.*
- *I have ears to hear what Father God is saying to me. He speaks to me all the time.*

PRAYER

Father God, thank you for your words of life and hope today. Breathe on me. Let the breath of your words saturate me bringing healing to my mind, emotions, body, soul, and spirit. I choose to look to you and to hold on to what I know to be true. I refuse to live by my feelings and invite the breath of you, my Father, to lift me above my circumstances and to cause me to look at today from your perspective. Thank you for what you are going to do in and through me.

DAY 10

You are my beloved child. I see you right where you are. I know everything about you and I love you. I see everything that no one else sees. I see what's hidden. I see those fears, those worries, those struggles, those unfulfilled hopes, those disappointments with yourself, others, and even with me and I still love you. I want you to let me take the weight of them today. Give them to me. Take my hand and walk with me. Let me show you my glory today. My glory shining into those hidden areas will cause you to lock eyes with me and change your perspective. I am yours and you are mine. NOTHING, absolutely NOTHING can change that truth. Walk in that truth today. I see you. I know you. I love you. My hand of blessing is on you today!

(Psalm 139)

DECLARATIONS

- *I am the workmanship of my Father.*
- *I am fearfully and wonderfully made.*

- *My Father's hand of blessing is on me today, leading and guiding from when I wake to when I go to sleep.*
- *I am prepared for good works, which the Father had in mind before I was formed in my mother's womb.*
- *My Father's thoughts of me are precious and I can't even count them. They outnumber the grains of sand.*

PRAYER

Father God, thank you that you are always with me. Thank you that I am your beautiful work of art and you've got plans for my life, which are good. I choose to embrace them. I know you will enable me to fulfil your purposes for my life. Thank you that there is nowhere I can go to hide from your presence. Thank you that you know me inside out and you still love me and desire me. I choose to believe this even though I don't always feel it. Thank you that your thoughts towards me are precious. Thank you that I am always on your mind. Thank you that you know the beginning from the end in my life and I can rest easy in your embrace.

DAY 11

Through my Son, Jesus Christ, you are 100% loved and worthy to receive all of my promises. There is no 'maybe', no 'let's see', and no 'small print'. They are yours if you're willing to receive them. Your freedom has been bought with a high price. You don't have to earn it. No one can take it from you. You are my beloved. Come, walk in all I have for you. Come, dance with me, today. Let me show you the life I have for you. You won't be disappointed. Come, draw near to me and I will draw near to you. Come. Come. Come. My promises are true and I am your faithful Father, your consistent Friend, your Comforter, your Guide, your Protector, your Shepherd, your Teacher, and your Rock. Come glean in my presence. Come and linger, take your time, and you will receive all that I have for you. I can't wait to bless you. I can't wait to pour out my favour on you. Come! Receive! You'll be richer for it.

(James 4:8)

DECLARATIONS

- *In Christ, I am 100% loved and worthy of all His spiritual blessings.*
- *As I draw near to my Father, He draws near to me.*
- *Father God never changes. He is the One who was, who is, and who is to come.*
- *Father God is faithful. I can trust everything He does.*
- *In Christ, I am blessed and highly favoured.*

PRAYER

Father God, thank you that I am 100% loved and accepted in Christ. I am worthy of all your spiritual blessings. Thank you that I am highly favoured and I have a victorious DNA in me. Thank you that you are faithful. You are consistent. You are my Comforter, my Guide, my Protector, my Teacher, my Rock, and my Good Shepherd. Thank you that because you are in me, I can carry your presence everywhere I go. I choose to linger in your presence today to receive all that you have for me.

DAY 12

Don't worry about anything. Instead give me what is worrying you today and in its place I will give you my peace. It will guard and protect your heart and mind today. If you only give me part of your worries, you won't be able to receive all of my peace. My peace exceeds anything you will ever understand or experience. My peace will see you through today. Resist the temptation to hold on to your worries trying to untangle them in your own strength. Hand them over to me. Little by little I will comb out the tangles for you. You can stand by and watch in peace. While you watch, give thanks and focus on what is true, honourable, right, pure, lovely, and admirable. As you do, more peace will be released into those very areas that caused you so much anxiety. I am your Father of peace and I will be with you today. Turn your eyes to me. Fix your thoughts on me and give thanks. Turn your worries to worship and they will become places of peace; places of praise; places your trust grows. Magnify me and your worries will seem small in comparison. Exalt me today and my Presence will be released in everything you face.

(Philippians 4:4-9)

DECLARATIONS

- *I am a worshipper of my Father.*
- *Worries don't consume me, worship does.*
- *Faith and strength arise as I worship.*
- *As I worship, Jesus is glorified, Heaven invades my now, and what is not of God shakes in terror.*
- *As I worship, I receive Heaven's perspective on my life. I begin to see things the way my Father does.*

PRAYER

Father, thank you that I have been created to worship you. Thank you for the gift of worship. When I worship, I bring you glory. When I worship the enemy flees. Thank you that faith and strength will rise in me as I worship you.

DAY 13

The greatest gift you will ever have is my Son living in you. He is enough for you. Everything else is just trimmings. Christ in you is your hope today. Christ in you allows you to share in my glory today. Rejoice that I am in you. Rejoice that I am around you. Rejoice that I will never leave you. Rejoice that nothing can separate you from my love today. Rejoice that I will show you the way of life. Rejoice that you will live with me forever. Rejoice that my presence brings hope, joy, life, and peace. Rejoice that I love you and I want the best for you. Rejoice!

(Psalm 16:11; Colossians 1:27)

DECLARATIONS

- *I choose to rejoice in the Lord.*
- *I am full of joy and hope because the Father is in me and I am in Him.*
- *Everywhere I go, I release joy and hope because I am a carrier of joy and hope.*
- *The joy of the Lord is my strength.*

- *Father God is the source of my hope - it will never run out.*

PRAYER

Father, thank you for Jesus. Thank you that He is my glory and the lifter of my head. Thank you that He is in me and everywhere I go I can release His joy and hope. I choose to surrender anything that will hinder your joy and hope in my life. I want to leak your joy and hope wherever I go. I rejoice in you. I am rich in you today. You are the kindest and most generous person I will ever know. Thank you, Father, that your resources will never run out. I will never be short of joy and hope as long as I look to you.

DAY 14

I am your loving Father and you are my beloved child. You don't need to hide your weakness from me. I see it and understand it. Remember, my faithful love endures forever. You don't need to be strong and have it all together before coming to me. Your weakness releases my love and my strength into your mess and confusion. Your weakness doesn't push me away. It draws me to you. I look for those I can strengthen. When you are weak, I am strong. When you are overwhelmed, I am peace. When you lack hope, I have enough for you. When you lack joy, your cup will overflow. My beloved child, don't be ashamed of the mess in your life. Allow my love to cover it. Your circumstances may not change but the way you see them and respond to them will be different. I am with you today in the midst of all that will get done and all that won't get done. Look for me in the mundane. Look for me in the hard. Look for me in the questions. Look for me in the disappointments. Look for me and you will find me. I am your encouragement and strength today. My faithful love will never fail you. My fingerprints of love are all around. Look for them and they will put a smile on your face.

(2 Chronicles 16:9; Psalm 89:11; 136; Isaiah 41:10)

DECLARATIONS

- *God's love never fails.*
- *Fingerprints of His love are all around me.*
- *They protect me, sustain me, guide me, and give me purpose.*
- *There's nothing like the pure, consistent, unfailing love of my Father.*
- *I can love today because He first loved me.*

PRAYER

Thank you, Father God, for your love. Thank you that your love is relentless, unstoppable, and unconditional. Thank you that your love never fails. Your love surrounds me and is my shield. Thank you that your love is perfect. Fear no longer has a hold on me because your love wins every time.

I delight in you today and I am singing over you: Come my beautiful one, sing with me. Worship me with your words, thoughts, and actions today. My unfailing love for you is always there. Nothing you hear today and nothing that is done to you today can take that away from you. As soon as you come to me, I will come to you and answer you. My strength is your encouragement. My glory surrounds you. My favour rests on you. I always have time for you. I see you. I am interested in all that goes on in your life. My powerful right hand will guide you today. It will protect you, save you, and care for you. I have made you. You are mine and I will never abandon you. I am working out my plans for your life today. For the honour of my name, I will finish what I have started and I will keep my promises. You can trust me, beloved child. You are safe in my hands today. I am carrying you through the storms of questions, disappointments, confusion, and hurt. Rather than focussing on what causes the storms in your life, focus on me, the One who calms the storm and is trustworthy. Focus on the One who will never leave you or forsake you.

(Psalm 138; 2 Corinthians 1:20)

DECLARATIONS

- *The Father delights in me today and sings over me.*
- *He calms my storms.*
- *I can trust Him and He will never abandon me.*
- *I walk in His glory and favour today.*
- *I can face today because I am safe in the Father's love and care for me. No one and nothing can rob me of His unfailing love.*

PRAYER

Father, thank you for your unfailing love. Thank you that you delight in me and sing over me. Thank you for your glory that surrounds me and your favour that rests on me everywhere I go. I choose to trust you in everything I face because I know you are trustworthy. I will no longer focus on my storms, questions, disappointments, confusion, and hurts. I will no longer understand their speech and listen to their lies. Instead, I choose to focus on you. My eyes are on you. Thank you that your strength is your gift to me. I receive it and I walk in it today.

My Son, Jesus, is alive! He is alive in you! This is life changing! Allow this truth to travel the 18 inches from your head to your heart and it will utterly transform the way you see today. It will change the way you live. Jesus, my one and only Son, is alive in you. Jesus is for you. Jesus is greater than anything you will face today. When you feel overwhelmed, look to Jesus. He is your Rock, your Refuge, your Strength. He knows the way you should go. He knows what you need every moment of every day. He will provide! Look to Him. Give yourself completely to Him today and my Spirit will lead you forward on a firm footing. Walking in the power of my Spirit will keep you firmly rooted and secure. No matter what you face today, you'll be able to stand because Jesus is alive in you and you have the power of my Spirit. The only way to experience open doors, hope, and breakthrough is to allow my life to consume every area of your life. All other attempts will only lead to disappointment. Give yourself to me. Your surrender and obedience will attract my favour and blessing today.

(Psalm 142 and 143)

DECLARATIONS

- *The same power that raised Jesus from the dead lives in me.*
- *I am alive in Christ and carry His power and authority everywhere I go.*
- *My surrender and obedience will attract Heaven and release His glory and favour on my life.*
- *Jesus is greater than anything I will face today.*
- *Jesus already knows what I need and will provide. I will want for nothing.*

PRAYER

Father, thank you for sending Jesus. Thank you that He not only came to save me but He wants to shape me into all that you want me to be by the power of your Spirit. Thank you that I am hidden in Christ. I am safe in Christ. I am complete in Christ. I am becoming like Christ. All my needs are met in your Son, Jesus Christ. Burn the truth of these words on my heart so that I will be forever transformed, walking in the power and authority of the King of kings and Lord of lords.

My child, come into my presence. You don't need to be afraid. You have free access all the time. I am never off duty. I never sleep. Don't let fear hold you back from coming into all I have for you. I am inviting you to come closer. Come with boldness. I have so much I want to tell you, so much I want to give you. Let me be part of everything you're doing today so that I can speak into your life. Put your confidence in me for everything. Put your hope in me. Then and only then will you experience an overflowing joy. I am the One who made everything. I am the One who keeps ALL His promises. I am the One who reigns. I am the One who gives justice to the oppressed and food to the hungry. I am the One who sets captives free, opens blind eyes, and lifts up those who are weighed down. You can trust me. I will use you today for my glory. Come closer. Have confidence in me. I never disappoint my children. I am your good Father. If you are willing, I will use you today to lift the oppressed and set captives free. As you put your trust in me, I will work in and through you releasing my heart to those around you. Listen carefully to me and let me guide you.

(Psalm 146)

DECLARATIONS

- *I come into my Father's presence with great confidence and boldness.*
- *I am tuned to Heaven today and I can clearly hear the words of my Father.*
- *I have the confidence to give away whatever the Father wants me to give to others. Freely I have received, freely I give.*
- *My hope is in the Lord and I will carry hope to others.*
- *The joy of the Lord is rising up in me and I will infect others with His joy.*

PRAYER

Father, thank you that you are my hope and my joy today. Thank you that I can come boldly into your presence and there receive all that I need. Thank you that you want to impart your words to me. I am listening. I want to be like Jesus where He only did what He saw you doing and only said what He heard you saying. I desire and long for that same kind of intimate relationship you had with your Son so that I can be more effective for your Kingdom. Thank you that my influence around me will increase as I learn to cherish those moments of intimacy in your presence. I choose to draw near to you. Thank you that you have promised to draw near to me as I draw near to you. Thank you that you will give me the desire and power to do what pleases you.

You are my chosen one, chosen for purpose. You are secure in my hands. I understand you and I know you. I see when you are hurting and when your heart is bleeding. My Son was hurt for you. He bled for you. Because of His scars, your scars will heal. Because of His scars, your scars will become a message of my goodness. Because of His scars, you can live in hope. My word secures your hope. I always keep my promises and am gracious in all I do. Look to me. The world says you can only have peace and joy when everything is going the way you want it to. I say you can have a deep-rooted peace and an overflowing joy in the midst of hurt and pain. I know it doesn't make sense, but step into my presence and find out for yourself. Look to me. Surrender to me and my peace and joy will surprise you. They will enable you to navigate the choppy waters of today. My peace and joy will give you purpose, perspective, and insight. My peace and joy will keep you from giving up. Call on me and I will draw close to you. Together we can accomplish the impossible today because I am the God of the impossible. Choose to focus on the possible rather than the impossible.

(Psalm 145)

DECLARATIONS

- *I am chosen for a purpose. Today has purpose for the Kingdom.*
- *My life is a message of the Father's goodness and kindness.*
- *Deep-rooted joy and peace will carry me and enable me to navigate everything that is thrown at me.*
- *Because I am chosen for purpose, my life has purpose.*
- *I will persevere and not give up for joy and peace that are set before me to see His Kingdom come and His will be done here on earth as it is in Heaven.*

PRAYER

Father, thank you that I can have deep-rooted peace and joy today. The roots of peace and joy will keep me from giving up. Thank you for the purpose I have in you. Thank you for the perspective you give me on life. Thank you for the insight and wisdom I need to fulfil your purpose. Thank you that I can join hands with you today and be part of seeing your Kingdom come to earth. Here I am. Take me. Use me. I am yours. Thank you that together we can accomplish the impossible because I am holding the hand of the One who brings possibilities to every situation.

Y ou are my tapestry of grace being woven in love. Surrender the threads of your life to me and I will create a masterpiece for my honour and glory. Don't pick and choose which colours to surrender. Surrender them all, the bright, the light, the beautiful, the dark, the dull, and the ugly. In my hands they will be used to weave the most beautiful design; a design I had in mind before you were even formed in your mother's womb. I am able to use both the good and the bad, the successes and the failures to create beauty. My hands are masterful at restoring, redeeming, and renewing. I delight in giving you beauty for your ashes. I delight in restoring the years the locusts have eaten. I delight in giving you a double blessing for every sorrow you have endured. I delight in giving you my garment of praise in exchange for your heaviness. Rejoice in me and your strength will rise. Praise me and you will experience my power. Look to me and you will receive direction. You are my tapestry of grace woven with great care and unfailing love. Trust me. Lean on me. I haven't finished weaving yet. I will finish what I have started in you for the honour and glory of my name.

(Ephesians 2:10; Philippians 1:6)

DECLARATIONS

- *My Father will complete the good work that He has started in me.*
- *My Father will give me beauty for my ashes.*
- *My Father will restore the years the locusts have eaten.*
- *My Father will give me a garment of praise and a crown of blessing.*
- *My Father is a God of restoration, redemption, and renewal. I am restored. I am redeemed. I am renewed. I will see what has been lost restored, redeemed, and renewed. I am taking back all that the enemy has stolen.*

PRAYER

Father, thank you that your grace and love are weaving my life into a beautiful tapestry for your honour and glory. Thank you that whatever I place in your hand is never wasted or discarded. Thank you that you can use everything to create something beautiful and significant as a testimony to your glory. I choose to surrender everything to you with confidence that you will do what only you can do. Thank you that in surrender there is no shame, only restoration, redemption, and renewal, leading to a life of beauty. Thank you that you will restore the years the locusts have eaten. In your power and grace, I choose to take back the ground the enemy has stolen. What has been taken will be restored and used powerfully to see your kingdom come.

DAY 20

I will be a shield around you today. Everything you experience today I can use for my glory and bring about my purposes in your life. I am your glory today. I am the One who holds your head high. Your circumstances don't affect my glory or the fact that I am holding you today. Let me lift your chin so you can lock eyes with me today. You will find yourself living from a place of victory. I won your victory once and for all. Victory is found in me and in no other place or person. You don't have to strive for victory. It is yours. You are free to live from a place of victory. My hand of blessing is on you today. Rest in that truth today. Allow it to empower you.

(Psalm 3)

DECLARATIONS

- *Father God is my glory and the lifter of my head today. I can walk with my head held high because He is holding me and fighting for me.*
- *Jesus has won my victory. I no longer need to strive for*

victory. It is mine in Christ Jesus - I am living from a place of victory.

- I can do all things today through Christ who empowers me and gives me strength.
- My eyes are locked with you, Father God. With my eyes on you nothing is too difficult or impossible.
- My Father never changes. He is always faithful, good, full of love, grace, and mercy.

PRAYER

Father, thank you that you are my glory and the lifter of my head. Thank you that as I lock eyes with you, strength and power will rise in me to accomplish all that you want me to do. Thank you, Jesus, that you won the victory on my behalf. I no longer need to fight or strive for it. Because you are in me and I am in you, I can confidently live from a place of victory today. Thank you that your hand is on me and I can just rest in all that I am and all that I have in you.

DAY 21

For The Lord delights in His people; He crowns the humble with victory!

— PSALM 149:4

I delight in you today. You are my precious child and it gives me great joy when you come to me and you enjoy my company. Humble yourself before me and I will give you victory in your thoughts and attitudes and breakthrough in your circumstances. As you acknowledge your need of me, I will help you to think like I do, to see what I see, and to have a heart that beats like mine. Tangled messes will no longer phase you. You will receive wisdom and revelation to deal with them in ways that will surprise you. I am your God. I am wisdom, revelation, and victory and I am in you. So, don't dwell on your weaknesses and inadequacies, rehearsing them again and again. That is not humility. Humility is acknowledging that you need someone greater than yourself to lead and guide you. Humility is living a life-style of praise and worship, lifting me up as the One who is greater. Humility is giving me your 'yes'. Humility will always draw Heaven to earth. You can sing for joy because I reign. You can shout for joy because I love you. You can jump for joy because I know you. You can live with joy because I have chosen you as my child. You are mine and I am yours.

(Proverbs 16:3)

DECLARATIONS

- *I humble myself before Almighty God and give Him my 'yes'.*
- *I have my Father's thoughts, I speak His words and do what He wants.*
- *My life is full of glory and favour because I humble myself before Almighty God.*
- *The Great I Am is in control of my life, filling me with power and strength to accomplish His purposes.*
- *The Great I Am is my source of everything.*

PRAYER

Father, thank you that nothing takes you by surprise. Nothing knocks you off your throne. I can completely rely on who you are and all that you do. I choose now to humble myself before you. I come into your presence to receive from you. Speak to me. Instruct me. I bless my ears to hear, my eyes to see, and my heart to understand. Thank you that as I humble myself, I receive your glory and favour. I choose to confidently walk in your glory and favour knowing it will be a testimony to your goodness today and in the days to come. I choose to live with joy and victory regardless of what I face.

DAY 22

Above all you must live as citizens of heaven...

— PHILIPPIANS 1:27

My child, you are forgiven. You are accepted. You are mine. I have placed you where you are to represent me. Heaven's values are your values. Wherever you are today you can radiate my love, joy, peace, purity, and hope because I am in you. You are full of my love, my joy, my peace, my purity, and my hope even if you don't feel like it. Because I am in you, I will flow through you wherever you put your feet today. You will bring love to the unloved. You will bring peace to the restless. You will bring joy to the sorrowing. You will bring hope to the hopeless. You are mine and you are radiating me wherever you go. Walk with me today. You are a citizen of my Kingdom living with my values for my honour and glory. Be content to bloom and flourish where I place you so that I can entrust more of myself to you. The more of me you have, the more you can give away; the more you will see my Kingdom come and the places you put your feet transformed. Rise up, my child, and represent me well. The opportunity to do today will never come to you again. Look to me and together we can do it well. Look to me and I will spread my fragrance and beauty through you.

DECLARATIONS

- *Jesus is alive in me and I am His representative.*
- *Father God leads me triumphantly.*
- *I am spreading the fragrance of Christ everywhere I go today.*
- *I walk in a manner worthy of the Lord and please Him in all that I do.*
- *Because we are one, I can bear fruit for His glory.*

PRAYER

Father, it is my honour and privilege to represent you as a citizen of Heaven. Thank you that I am not where I am by chance but you have placed me where I am to bloom and flourish. I choose to make space for more of you in my life today so that I can release your glory. Thank you that when I need love, joy, peace, and hope, I can just look to you because you are all that and more. In you, I have everything I need to walk as a citizen of Heaven where you have placed me. Thank you that you never require but you always enable as I choose to surrender to you. I surrender now and receive your enabling power to represent Heaven well today.

Jesus is alive. He is your hope today. He is your Prince of peace today. My Son came to earth and sacrificed everything to give you the gift of peace. This perfect peace can only be found in Him. He is peace personified. He embodies peace, breathes peace, and releases peace. His peace is here now - breathe it in. Breathe out your worries and breathe in His peace. Breathe out your disappointments and breathe in His peace. Breathe out your resentment, your grudges, your anger and breathe in His peace. His peace will enable you to see like I do, to hear like I do, to act like I would. Come to me today just as you are. I will give you peace in every situation you face. My peace is available in the midst of confusion, questions, disappointments, and frustrations, because I am right in the middle of all that you are experiencing. I am always with you. I will never leave you. My peace is always with you. My peace will never leave you. Reach out and receive it. I will keep you in perfect peace as you look to me. I will keep you in perfect peace as you keep your mind on me. I will keep you in perfect peace as you put your trust in me. Enjoy the gift of my peace today.

(Isaiah 26:3; John 14:27; 2 Thessalonians 3:16)

DECLARATIONS

- *Jesus is my Prince of Peace today.*
- *I choose to partner with my Prince of Peace today and to no longer listen to the speech of disappointment, resentment, grudges, anger, frustrations, confusion or worries. I will no longer understand their language.*
- *God is not a God of confusion but a God of order and peace.*
- *Peace rules in my heart today because I am focussed on my Father and I trust in Him.*
- *Nothing will rob me of this peace that I have received as a gift today.*

PRAYER

Father God, thank you that you are a God of peace and not a God of confusion. Thank you that I can breathe you in today and everything I do, say, and think will be influenced by your peace. I receive your peace today. Thank you that your peace surrounds me and guards what I think, say, and do. With a heart of peace, I can climb every mountain. Thank you that every time I put my trust in you, there is more peace to receive. I choose to do that now.

DAY 24

M y child, I have you safe in my hands today. I see you. You are mine. I am carrying and supporting you today with my victorious right hand. You don't need to be afraid. You don't need to be discouraged. I am your God. I have won the victory for you. I am everything you need today. I am in control. I am for you and I am working everything out for your good. Nothing is wasted with me. Nothing is futile. Nothing is impossible. I am your strength today. I am your help today. I am all you need. I am enough. I will never leave you on your own - I am always there. Call on me today. Trust me today. I will spread my protection over you and fill you with joy; a deep-rooted joy that comes from trusting me and doesn't depend on your circumstances. Your circumstances don't dictate your joy and peace. Trusting me releases joy and peace. Call on me! Trust me! Let me surprise you.

(Psalm 5; Isaiah 41:10)

DECLARATIONS

- *Because the Lord is at my right hand today, I will not be shaken.*
- *Underneath me are the everlasting arms of Father God supporting me and carrying me.*
- *God is the God of the impossible.*
- *Nothing placed in the hands of my loving Father is ever wasted.*
- *My strength comes from the One who is almighty and full of power. He never grows weary.*

PRAYER

Father, thank you that I am safe in your hands. Nothing will ever snatch me from you. Thank you that you will never get tired of carrying me. You will never set me down and leave me to cope on my own. I look to you and I trust you today. Thank you that you are my strength and my help. Thank you that as I look to you and trust you the joy and peace I receive will grow strong roots and not be taken from me. I am rooted in you, safe and secure. I look forward to your surprises for me today. Thank you that today is another adventure in your Kingdom.

When the storms of life come... the godly have a lasting foundation.

— PROVERBS 10:25

Don't let the storms unsettle you because they will come. It's not a matter of 'if' but 'when'. I have given you all you need to navigate each and every one. They don't need to throw you off course. Your solid and unshakable foundation is my Son Jesus. He is your Rock and Refuge. He is the cornerstone on which to build your life. He is your hope. My Son, everything He is, everything He accomplished for you, is my love gift to you. Receive Him. Walk with Him and you will experience the only stronghold that will see you through every storm. He is your anchor - your spiritual lifeline. Anchored to Him you will not only survive the storms but also thrive in them. Take heart because the storms you weather in my power will allow me to keep adding brushstrokes of beauty to the canvas of your life. Each stroke has meaning. Each stroke has purpose. Each stroke produces character. Look to me. Let me give you my perspective on what is going on in your life today. Remember, I haven't finished my work in you yet.

(Hebrews 6:19)

DECLARATIONS

- *I am firmly planted on my Rock and will thrive today and not merely survive.*
- *In Christ I have the greatest gift of all.*
- *Every spiritual blessing and benefit is mine through Christ.*
- *Jesus is the anchor of my soul keeping me securely tied to all that Father God has for me so that I can thrive in the storms of life.*
- *The name of the Lord is my strong tower. I run to it and am kept safe.*

PRAYER

Father, thank you that when the storms come, I don't need to panic or worry. At the name of Jesus every knee will bow. I speak to the storms I am facing today and say they will bow to the name of Jesus. I will no longer partner with them and allow them to control who I am. They do not define me. You control me. You define me. There's power in the name of Jesus to calm the storms today. Thank you that you give me the strength, wisdom, and the know-how to weather the storms that come my way. Thank you that what was meant for evil, you turn around and create something beautiful, enhancing who I am, giving meaning and purpose to my life. I look to you and trust you. I will not be overwhelmed because you have everything I need. Thank you, Father.

You are my prized possession, my joy. Instead of striving today, just submit to me. It's in submitting that you find peace. Tune into my voice today. Treasure my instructions. Store them up in your heart. Look to me and delight yourself in me. I'm not looking for impressive words. I'm not even looking for wonderful works. I'm looking for your heart. It's not about performance. It's about relationship. It's about surrender. It's about placing your life into my hands. When I have your heart everything else will naturally fall into place. Come to me and surrender. Come to me and enjoy my company. In that place of surrender and intimacy you will find your true identity. You will find true success. You will find direction. You will find peace. You will find contentment. You will find fulfilment. Come to me. Hold my hand today and walk with me. My light will shine on the road ahead of you. Together we can make today work for my glory! Together we can have influence on those around you. I love you with an everlasting, unfailing love and I want to see you succeed today.

(Job 22:21, 22, 28).

DECLARATIONS

- *I am a crown of glory and a royal diadem in the hand of the Lord.*
- *Father God rejoices over me with gladness and singing. His love quiets my heart.*
- *I choose to trust Him and lean on Him, instead of my own understanding.*
- *Father God has chosen me for Himself as His special treasure.*
- *Father God instructs me and keeps me as safe as I surrender to Him.*

PRAYER

Father, thank you that I am your crown of glory and a royal diadem in your hand. Thank you that you rejoice over me with singing. You see me as the apple of your eye. I am important to you. Father, I choose to surrender to you because I know your desire for me is for good. I love keeping company with you. I want to influence those around me as my intimacy with you grows. Thank you that your words will instruct my heart. Your words are a lamp to my feet and a guide to my path. Thank you that you love me for who you made me and I don't need to be anyone else. I choose to humble myself before you today and enter into that beautiful relationship you long to see me enjoy. I love you .

Come to me my beloved. I want to be your refuge today where you can find safety. In me you will find safety from the winds of people's opinions; safety from disappointing and unresolved situations; safety from worries and questions, blowing around and creating chaos. Surrender to me and you will receive safety. Let me be your Master today. Every good thing you have comes from my hand. Give thanks! I am your inheritance. You don't need to worry about your future. Surrender! Your cup will overflow with my blessings. Surrender! I will richly supply everything you need. Not just barely, but richly. Surrender! I am the one who will guide you. I will instruct your heart even at night and give you ideas, divine strategies, and insight. Surrender! I will always be with you. Because I am at your right hand, you will never be shaken. I will never leave you on your own. Surrender! I will show you how to live. In my presence you will find joy. Surrender! You are mine and I am yours. I will not disappoint you. I am your good, good Father.

(Psalm 16; Acts 2:25)

DECLARATIONS

- *I am confident that I will see the Lord's goodness while I am here in the land of the living.*
- *The Lord will protect me when troubles come. He will place me out of reach on a high rock.*
- *I can walk with my head held high because fear has no grip on me.*
- *The Lord will teach me how to live. He will lead me along the right path.*
- *I walk with creative ideas, insights, and divine strategies today because the Father has given them to me.*

PRAYER

Father, thank you that I can come to you at any time and experience safety. Thank you that in your presence the things the enemy would like to throw at me cannot stick. I choose to think of things that are excellent and worthy of praise. Thank you that when I worship you, Heaven opens and I receive creative ideas, insights, and divine strategies leading me into all the blessings you have for me. Father, thank you that you love to give good gifts. You are the most loving and generous Father.

My dear child, because you are united with my Son, you are complete. You are whole. Nothing can change that. That is how I see you. Don't focus on what you lack. Focus on all that you are and all that you have in me. Rejoice in my strength. Celebrate my hope, peace, and victory today. I want to give you your heart's desire. I will withhold no good thing from you. Come to me. Enter my rest. Enter that place where you are one with me and all your fears and worries will fade away because I am perfect love. My perfect love eliminates fear. My perfect love will keep you from stumbling today, in your thoughts, words, and actions. Receive my perfect love. I want you to feel comfortable in my love today. Rejoice that you are 100% loved and worthy to receive all of my blessings.

(Psalm 21 and 34; Colossians 2:9-10)

DECLARATIONS

- *Father God loves me with an everlasting love and has promised to give me a future and a hope.*

- *He has drawn me to Himself and will give me the desires of my heart. No good thing will He withhold from me as I focus on Him and put my trust in Him.*
- *The Father's banner over me today is love.*
- *I am rooted in the love of God and am made complete through Jesus Christ.*
- *I am an object of His deepest love and affection.*

PRAYER

Father, thank you for your love. Thank you that your everlasting love surrounds me and gives me a future and a hope. Thank you that you have drawn me to yourself and I can be assured that you will withhold no good thing from me as I lean on you and put my trust in you. Thank you that in Christ I am made whole. I rejoice in all that I am and all that I have in you. I choose to receive your perfect love. It enables me to stand firm and not be shaken like a tree firmly rooted in the ground. Thank you that I am an object of your deepest love and affection. Thank you that your banner over me today is love.

I am your good Shepherd, not just any shepherd but One who knows you. The One who loves you, who will provide for you, and who cares deeply for you. No child of mine is treated like an orphan. You are my beautiful child and you will lack nothing today. Look to me and walk in all that is rightfully yours. You don't need to beg. You just need to receive. In my presence you will find rest today. In my presence your strength will be renewed. I will lead you today with my unfailing love. My love will chase away all your fears and anxieties. My love is a perfect love. It surrounds you today. It protects you today. Receive my perfect love. Wear it, walk in it, and allow it to transform you from the inside out. You have the honour and the privilege of bringing glory to my name today. My love and my goodness will always follow you. My love and my goodness will support you. My love and my goodness have got your back. You cannot run away from my love and goodness. Nothing will come between you and my love. My love is relentless! My love is unstoppable!

(Psalm 23; Romans 8:31-39; Ephesians 1-3)

DECLARATIONS

- *The Lord is my good Shepherd. I will want for nothing.*
- *I have been given the spirit of adoption and am called a child of God.*
- *The Lord's love and goodness surround me today and follow me always.*
- *I wear the garment of perfect love today and everything I think, say, and do will be influenced by Father God's perfect love.*
- *I live a life of perfect love. Fear has no place in me.*

PRAYER

Father, thank you that you are my good Shepherd. You care for me like no one else. Thank you that I can trust you to know me, love me, and to provide for me every single day. I have no reason to worry or to be anxious. Thank you that I belong to you. I am accepted in you, through Christ. I have been chosen in Christ before the foundation of the world to be holy and blameless before you. Thank you that this isn't something that is out of my reach. Your love, your grace, and your mercy have made this accessible to me now. I can live a holy and blameless life before you today as I allow you to support me with your perfect love. I receive your perfect love. I choose to wear it as a testimony to your grace and mercy. Father, you are so good and I love you. Thank you that as I receive your love, I will be able to love you more. Glorify yourself through me today.

DAY 30

Open wide the doors and gates to the situations you are facing today and let me, your King of glory, come in. One touch from me, one glance from me, one breath from me, one word from me will change everything. In my presence you will always be changed from glory to glory. I am the Lord strong and mighty. I am the One who wins every battle. Trust me today. You will never be disgraced. Open wide your doors and gates and let me, the King of glory, come in. I will lead you with unfailing love and faithfulness. Put your hope in me. I am accomplishing my purposes in your life today. Put your hope in me and you won't feel like giving up. Put your hope in me and today will take the shape I want. Open wide those doors and gates and let me in. Together we can make it today. Together we will make a difference. You and I are a majority.

(Psalm 24 and 25)

DECLARATIONS

- *Father God gives me victory through Jesus Christ my Lord.*

- *Father God leads me triumphantly today.*
- *I abound in grace and carry the glory of my Father.*
- *Because I have put my hope in the Lord, I will not be disgraced.*
- *Father has delivered me from the power of darkness and has transferred me into the kingdom of His dear Son. The evil one cannot touch me.*

PRAYER

Father, thank you that one touch, one glance, one breath from you changes everything. Thank you that I don't need to rely on my own strength but I can look to you. I choose to open the doors to whatever I face today and invite you to come in with all your glory and power. I give you control. I surrender to you. You have permission to reign over me, my home, and my circumstances. I declare you are LORD of this day. I choose to walk in obedience bringing honour and glory to your name.

You are my chosen one; a royal priest. You are all mine. You are secure in my hands. You are complete in me through my Son. You have the power within you to bring light to all the dark places today because you have my Spirit living in you. Because I have chosen you, because you are my possession, you can show others my goodness today. Walk as a chosen one today. Walk as a carrier of my goodness and glory today. Once you had no identity. But now you are my glory-carrying child. You are my chosen, royal child living for my glory. You are my precious possession. Let's walk in complete unity, today. Let my thoughts be your thoughts. Let my words be your words. Then and only then will you be able to bring out my colours and my flavours around you. Without me you can do nothing. But with me you can do the unimaginable, the impossible. Hold your head high and walk with me.

(1 Peter 2:9-10; Matthew 5)

DECLARATIONS

- *I am a chosen one of Almighty God, my Father. I am royalty.*
- *I am His and He is mine. We are one.*
- *I am His light shining brightly in a dark world. The darkness around me cannot put out the light He has put in me.*
- *Because I belong to the Father, I have identity.*
- *The same power that raised Jesus from the dead lives in me and is working in and through me today.*

PRAYER

Father God, thank you that I am yours. Thank you for choosing me and giving me the title of royal priest. Thank you that because you are in me and I am in you, I have the power to bring light and hope to all the dark and hopeless situations I encounter today. Let your light shine brightly in me. I root myself in your love today so that I can walk with boldness and courage and accomplish all that you would like me to do. Empower me to bring out your colours and flavours everywhere I go. Thank you that you are the God of the impossible. I choose to take your hand today, to walk with you, to work with you and I know you will surprise me with what you can do. I look to you and trust you.

My precious child, reach out to me today. I want to be merciful to you today. Receive my mercy. I want to bless you today. Receive my blessings. You are my beloved and I have so much I want to share with you. Come to me and let me reveal my kindness and goodness to you. Draw near to me and listen to what I have for you. I want to share my secrets with you today. We are one. Come close and enjoy my presence. Allow me to be part of all you do today. I love being with you. I smile with favour on you, my beautiful child, because you are created in our image. Sing for joy and you will be a carrier of my joy today. This over-flowing joy will yield a harvest for my glory. Come, my beautiful one, and enter into all I have for you today.

(Psalm 67)

DECLARATIONS

- *I bless my ears to hear what the Father has to say to me.*
- *I bless my heart to receive the secrets He wants to reveal to me.*

- *I bless my mouth to speak the words He wants me to speak.*
- *I am His joy carrier and my feet bring good news to those I meet.*
- *I am blessed abundantly with every spiritual blessing that comes from being one with Christ.*

PRAYER

Father, thank you for Jesus. Thank you that through Him I am blessed with every spiritual blessing in the heavenly realms. Thank you that you want to share your secrets with me. I am listening. Let me walk with your heartbeat today. Let me carry your love to a broken world. Thank you for your kindness. Thank you for your goodness. Thank you for the joy that I have in you. I choose to partner with your love, your kindness, your goodness, and to carry your joy everywhere I go today. Thank you that nothing I face today can rob me of the joy I have in you. I choose to rejoice in you today because the joy I have in you is the strength that will carry me through each moment. Thank you, Lord.

My child, my whispers of truth will keep your hearts soft. Cynicism, sarcasm, grudges, and resentment are always hovering trying to get into your heart. They want hopelessness and discouragement to rule your life. Only in my presence will your heart stay soft and open to all I have for you. Remember, I am for you, not against you. I know your sin and yet I call you by your name, not by your sin. I am the only one who can lift the weight of guilt and shame and lead you into a full, abundant life of favour and honour. You are my chosen child. You are not a mistake. You are fearfully and wonderfully made. Nothing is hidden from me. I see everything and I still love you with an everlasting love. I invite you to come boldly into my presence where you will find everything you need. Hold on tightly to all that I am without any wavering. I am your hope today. I will keep my promises. Don't throw away your trust in me. It is in trusting me that you will find a way forward moment by moment, hour by hour, and day by day. You won't drown in the storms of life. I am with you and I will see you through each and every one. I am about to do something new in your life. Receive it with an open and a soft heart. I will make a pathway through your wilderness. I will create rivers in your dry wastelands. You are my chosen child and in my presence you will be restored, refreshed and renewed.

(Isaiah 43; Hebrews 4:6-16; 10:19-39)

DECLARATIONS

- *I am fearfully and wonderfully made.*
- *I am in Christ and in Him there is no condemnation. I may experience conviction but condemnation is not of Him.*
- *Shame has no hold on me. I am free to be all that God has made me to be.*
- *I am a new creation; Father God is doing a new thing in and through me.*
- *He is restoring me, refreshing me, and renewing me today.*

PRAYER

Father, thank you that I am fearfully and wonderfully made for your glory. I am not a mistake. Thank you that your Spirit only convicts and never condemns. I will no longer partner with shame, guilt, cynicism, sarcasm, grudges, resentment, hopelessness, or discouragement. They have no place in my life. I repent, turn from them, and turn to you. Thank you for forgiveness and grace. Thank you for your restoration, refreshing, and renewal. In you I find a pathway in my wilderness and rivers in my wastelands. Thank you that you are doing a new thing in and through me. I receive it.

DAY 34

My word for you today is TRUST ME! TRUST ME! TRUST ME! Put your trust in me and find the place of rest. It's in trusting that you find rest. It's in trusting that you find purpose. It's in trusting that life makes sense. My word is always true and you can trust everything I do. It's in trusting that hope will sustain you and peace will carry you. TRUST ME TODAY! I am your help and your shield. My unfailing love surrounds you. I look down from heaven and can see you. I made you and I understand everything about you. You are safe in me. So TRUST ME!

(Psalm 33:4,13-15,20-22)

DECLARATIONS

- *I trust in the Lord with all my heart and I won't lean on my own understanding.*
- *The Lord is faithful and His love endures forever.*
- *The Lord is my strength and my song. He gives me victory.*

- *The strong right arm of the Lord will do glorious things in and through me.*
- *The Lord is God and He is shining on me today, giving me success in all that I do for His glory and honour.*

PRAYER

Father, thank you that you are trustworthy. You will never deceive or disappoint me. I can trust you completely. Thank you that you are faithful. Thank you that your love endures forever. Thank you that you are my strength and my song today. I have reason to sing because you bring victory in every situation as I choose to trust in you.

Remember who I am. I can cause all things to work together for your good. When I say all things, I mean ALL things, not just the things you think might work together for your good. All things. Those things that seem like hurdles, those things that stand like mountains of impossibilities, those regrets, those disappointments, those failures. Give them to me and I will shape them into something beautiful for your good. Precious child, in my hands your life is always safe and secure. Lean on me. Trust me. Put your whole weight on me and allow me to do what only I can do. Remember, I have chosen you and called you to myself. Stop living as though you were your own. I have given you right standing with myself. Stop striving for something you already are and have. I have given you my glory. Stop allowing things around you to cover up the glory I have given you. Come out of hiding today and shine brightly for the honour of my name. I love you. You are my precious, prized possession. I am with you.

(Romans 8:28-30)

DECLARATIONS

- *All things will work together for my good today because I love the Lord and am called according to His purpose.*
- *Father God is shaping me moment by moment to become more like His Son Jesus.*
- *Father God knew me in advance and chose me. I am His chosen child.*
- *Father God has given me His glory. I am His glory carrier today.*
- *I have right standing with the Father because of Jesus.*

PRAYER

Father, thank you that there is nothing in my life that you can't turn around and change for good. You love giving beauty for ashes. I give you my ashes today and look forward to what you are going to do in and through them. Thank you that everything I experience can make me more like your Son Jesus so that I can shine brightly for your glory. I choose to come out of hiding today. I will no longer partner with things that will hide your glory. You have permission to shine in me and to shine through me so the world can see your glory. I desire to bring honour to your name. Thank you that I have right standing with you because of Jesus. Thank you for knowing me and choosing me in advance so that I can be your glory carrier. I receive the mission with great joy. I can't think of anything better than to bring honour to your name. Be glorified in and through me today.

DAY 36

Come to me, my beloved. Be aware of my presence today. My presence is your protection today. My presence provides shelter from stormy thoughts. My presence will calm your fears and worries even in the midst of questions and uncertainties. Trust me with your life today and you will experience my faithfulness in everything you face. Run to me. Trust me. Declare that I Am your God and your future is in my hands. Look up and my favour will shine on you. Look up and I will put a smile on your face. Look up and I will show you the wonders of my unfailing love. Hope in me today and you will receive strength and courage moment by moment. I am here for you. COME! I desire to walk with you today. Let me in and let me surprise you, my precious child. I have always loved you and I will never stop loving you. I am yours and you are mine. You are safe in my presence today.

(Psalm 31)

DECLARATIONS

- *You, O Lord, are my God. My future is in your hands.*
- *I fix my eyes on you, Lord, the One who initiates and perfects my faith.*
- *Weariness has no place in me as I look to you.*
- *As I look to you, I take a new grip with my tired hands and strengthen my weak knees.*
- *You enable me to mark out a straight path so others around me who are weak will not fall but become strong.*

PRAYER

Father, thank you that you are my God and my future is in your hands. Thank you, Jesus, that you are my champion. You have gone before me and you are the One who initiates and perfects my faith. As I come into your presence today, Father, I choose to strip off every weight that is tripping me up and slowing me down. I choose to run with endurance the race you have set before me. Thank you that I can come to you at any time and in any place. I choose to walk with you and to hope in you. Thank you for the strength and courage that come as a result of walking with you and hoping in you. I can't wait to see how you're going to surprise me. I bless my eyes to see your fingerprints of love, goodness, and faithfulness in my life.

I am not intimidated by evil, in fact I laugh at it. My child, when you hear a lie from the enemy, when you experience an attack, you don't need to run in fear. Do what I do and laugh. I am your strength. I am your fortress. I am your stronghold. The enemy is not!! I will stand with you and my unfailing love always surrounds you. Praise will increase your strength. Praise makes me your powerful stronghold. Sing about my power. Sing about my unfailing love. I am your refuge, your place of safety. My banner over you is love. You can run at your Goliaths today with confidence. Don't empower the lies that are thrown at you by rehearsing them and dwelling on them. Laugh at them, sing for joy, and they will become weak. They will have no power over you. I am in you and I am much greater than the enemy. He has no authority over you. You have my power and my authority. Walk in that truth today.

(Psalm 59)

DECLARATIONS

- *I don't have a spirit of fear but of love, power, and self-discipline.*
- *The battles I face have already been won for me in Christ. I am not fighting for victory. I am fighting from a place of already having won.*
- *I can now run at my Goliaths with joy and laughter because God is in me and He is bigger than any of my Goliaths.*
- *I am a God-pleaser and not a man-pleaser.*
- *I can take risks today in Jesus' name.*

PRAYER

Father, thank you for the spirit of love, power, and self-discipline you have given me. Thank you that I can laugh at the evil around me. I do not need to be intimidated by it. Thank you that you are my strength and my fortress, my stronghold. The Goliaths I face today will not defeat me because my eyes are on you. Thank you that the weapon you give me to use against them is praise, song, and worship. I praise you. I sing a new song to you. I worship you. Thank you that the battles I face have already been won. I am living from a place of victory. I choose to walk in the authority and power that you give me.

My dear child, delight yourself in me and I will give you the desires of your heart. As you come to me and enjoy my presence, my desires will become your desires. My thoughts will become your thoughts. My ways will become your ways. Your heart will beat with the same heartbeat I have. My presence is the safest place to be. You don't need to be afraid of it. Learn to enjoy it. Learn to practice it. Learn to host it. For the sake of those around you, learn to remain in me as I am in you so that your life will make a difference. Regardless of how you are feeling today, trust me, hope in me, praise me, and worship me. This is not being fake but living full of faith. I am drawn to lives of faith. I reward lives of faith. You will experience all I have for you just by delighting yourself in me. Enjoy me as your Father, Friend, Deliverer, Good Shepherd, Healer, Provider, Refuge, and Stronghold. Faith will flow from delighting in me. Without faith you cannot please me. Delight in me today and you will grow in your faith.

(Proverbs 3:5-6; Hebrews 11)

DECLARATIONS

- *God is my Father, Friend, Deliverer, and Good Shepherd.*
- *He is my Healer, Provider, Refuge, and Stronghold.*
- *I am a person of faith and I choose to delight myself in the Lord.*
- *Because of Jesus, I can live life with an overflowing joy. In His presence there is fullness of joy.*
- *I am chosen, anointed and appointed to go and produce lasting fruit. I can ask for anything in the name of Jesus and the Father will grant it.*

PRAYER

Father, thank you for the powerful name of Jesus. Thank you for the power there is in His name. Thank you that as I delight myself in you, you will give me the desires of my heart. Thank you that as I learn to walk with you, dance with you, do life with you, my desires will become your desires. We will become one as I choose to remain in you. Together we can make a difference as faith continues to rise in me. Lord, I believe, help my unbelief.

You are my precious treasure. Let me be your precious treasure today. I am your strength today. I am your shield today. You can trust me with all your heart. I am your faithful God. I will help you and fill your heart with joy. I want to give you a new song today. So burst out in song. Sing your songs of thanksgiving. Sing your songs of praise. I love to hear them. Never give up singing. Your songs will release faith and joy wherever you go. Your songs will release my presence. I love to come and be part of the praises my children sing.

(Psalm 28)

DECLARATIONS

- *I am first a worshipper of God and then a worker.*
- *Like David, I am a woman/man after God's own heart and I will sing songs of praise, thanksgiving, and worship in every situation.*
- *The songs I sing today will release faith and joy.*

- *My heart is filled with joy and I burst out in songs of thanksgiving.*
- *Great is the Lord and greatly to be praised.*

PRAYER

Father, you are great and greatly to be praised. I sing for joy to you, O Lord. I magnify you and exalt you above everything else in my life. I praise you with all that I am. Your word holds true and I can trust everything that you do. Your glory and unfailing love fill the earth. Great are you, Lord. You are full of power, love, glory, splendour, and majesty. You reign. I shout for joy, O Lord. I worship you with gladness. You are good and your unfailing love continues forever, your faithfulness to each generation. All praise, honour, glory, and power be to you forever and ever.

DAY 40

M y child, my presence is the most important thing you can ever experience in life. When you step into my presence, you receive your true identity. When you soak in my presence, you grow in my love and grace. When you rest in my presence, you find true protection from every lie, fear, and temptation that will try to derail you. When you are saturated with my presence, you receive power. It's in my presence that the truth of who I am becomes real to you. When my truth becomes real to you, you are more likely to walk in it. Remember, my child, you are always safe in my arms. I will never get tired of carrying you. I will never lose my grip on you. I will never drop you. I will never put you down. In my arms you are safe and secure; you are whole and complete. In my arms your life will make sense. In my arms you have all that you need. In my arms you can accomplish all that I have planned for you. You are my beautiful work of art and I am proud of you.

My presence is the safest place on earth.

DECLARATIONS

- *I am not living in my own strength but in the power of the Spirit.*
- *I can rest in my Father's presence and there find all that I need.*
- *I choose to walk in the light of my Father's presence today.*
- *My Father's presence is always with me, guiding, instructing, enabling, and providing.*
- *I am who God says I am. I can do what He says I can do.*

PRAYER

Father, thank you for the gift of your presence. I cherish it. I want to be a carrier of it every day of my life. Thank you that in your presence I have all that I need. In your presence is joy, truth, power, insight, love, wisdom, grace, mercy, forgiveness, revelation, and so much more. Everything that Heaven represents is found in your presence. Open my eyes to see. Open my ears to hear. Open my heart to perceive and understand. Thank you that I am who you say I am and I can do what you say I can do. I am yours. Use me to see your Kingdom come and your will be done here as it is in Heaven. Glorify yourself in and through me.

ABOUT THE AUTHOR

 Paige Squirrell is a writer, coach and leader. She has a passion to see God's Presence released in the lives of ordinary people bringing them to a place of real freedom. Paige longs to see people adopt a meaningful Kingdom lifestyle that brings joy and peace. Together with her husband Jonathan she co-leads Kingdom Breakthrough Ministries: equipping and releasing God's people everywhere.

She loves being a wife and has found real joy in raising four children. She recently became a grandmother and enjoys every minute of it.

Paige is a licensed minister of The Apostolic Network of Global Awakening and a regional consultant for the Filling Station Trust in East Anglia and London, UK.

facebook.com/kingdombreakthroughministries